PAPER WONDERLAND

PAPER WONDERLAND

32 Terribly Cute Toys Ready to Cut, Fold & Build

Michelle Romo

HOW BOOKS

Cincinnati, Ohio
www.howdesign.com

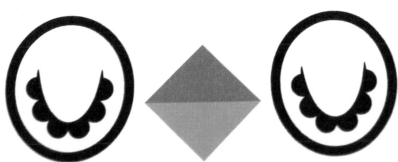

For more excellent books and resources for designers, visit
www.howdesign.com.

14 13 12 11   5 4 3 2

Distributed in Canada by Fraser Direct
100 Armstrong Avenue
Georgetown, Ontario, Canada L7G 5S4
Tel: (905) 877-4411

Distributed in the U.K. and Europe by David & Charles
Brunel House, Newton Abbot, Devon, TQ12 4PU, England
Tel: (+44) 1626-323200, Fax: (+44) 1626-323319
E-mail: postmaster@davidandcharles.co.uk

Distributed in Australia by Capricorn Link
P.O. Box 704, Windsor, NSW 2756 Australia
Tel: (02) 4577-3555

Library of Congress Cataloging-in-Publication Data

Romo, Michelle.
  Paper wonderland / Michelle Romo. -- 1st ed.
      p. cm.
  ISBN 978-1-60061-696-9 (pbk. : alk. paper)
  1. Paper work. I. Title.
  TT870.R576 2010
  745.54--dc22
                    2009043011

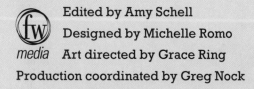

Edited by Amy Schell
Designed by Michelle Romo
Art directed by Grace Ring
Production coordinated by Greg Nock

ABOUT THE AUTHOR

Michelle Romo is a self-taught illustrator and designer who is fueled by cookies and naps. She got her first computer when she was sixteen, and she hasn't stopped working since. Her influences include Mid-Century, Japanese and Scandinavian design and pretty much anything cute.

Michelle created her line, Crowded Teeth, in 2004 and continues to create characters and products under that name. When she isn't working, she spends her time eating good food, hugging her friends, playing video games and crafting. She currently resides in Los Angeles with her husband, Jason, and their two cats, Hurts and Morgan.

THANK YOU!!!

This book is dedicated to my family!

I love you all and would be more of a crazy person
without your love and general awesomeness!

Mommy and Daddy
(Akiko & Ray)

Patrese and Raymond
(Sister & Nephew)

Grama and Papa
(Dorothy & Ray)

Bachan and Jichan
(Teruko & Kasui)

and last but not least . . .

J.
(My Favorite Person Ever)

Special thanks to Megan, Grace and Amy for all their help on my first book.

TABLE OF CONTENTS

What to Expect

Get ready to go on the paper adventure of a lifetime in the wonderful world of *Paper Wonderland*!

From the moment you step foot in the Neighborhood, you'll meet new friends who are ready to stick with you forever! You'll go hiking through the Forest with the woodland creatures and then relax with a dip in the Ocean. Next, you'll trade your beach towel for a safari hat when you go on a Jungle adventure that will knock your socks off! Finally, no trip is complete without taking a drive through the Big City and taking in some fabulous sites!

Come on! Let's go travel the world of *Paper Wonderland* and make some friends along the way!

What You'll Need to Get Started

I'm so excited you're here! Let's start this party! All of supplies you'll need for each paper toy are listed on the instruction pages. Just look for the section on the first page of each toy that looks like this:

You won't need more than scissors, double-sided tape and glue for most projects!

For a few of the toys, you may want some extra goodies like pipe cleaners and twine, but if you don't have these, don't worry. You'll just have to get creative with your building! I'll bet you can find something around the house that will make your toy even better!

General Tips on Making the Toys

All of the toys are very fun and easy to build! If you want to be a total expert, here are a few more tools that will help you on your way:

⅛" hole punch, ¼" hole punch, ruler, cutting knife and a pencil.

All of these items can be found in the school supply section of most stores.

The hole punches make cutting out tiny circles much easier and neater than using scissors to poke a hole. If you want really straight and clean edges, a ruler and a cutting knife are the way to go! Also, you can score the dotted lines by lightly using the knife. This will make for a cleaner fold. Having a pencil handy is always good idea! You can use it to hold things in place or to reach into tiny places.

Remember, you don't need these items! As long as you have scissors and tape, you should be ready to go!

Download Free Templates

And don't forget that after you make the toys in these pages, you can go to www.mydesignshop.com/wonderland to download free PDFs of the templates that appear in this book. That way, you can print out more templates and make more friends!

LET'S START THE ADVENTURE!

THE NEIGHBORHOOD

THE NEIGHBORHOOD

It's nice to meet you! I see you're moving into the house down the street. The cute one with the orange roof! We're going to have fun playing games and going on adventures. This is just the beginning!

WELCOME
TO THE NEIGHBORHOOD

Hey! Hi! Hello! Come in, come in!
We're all friends here and will do our best to make you feel welcome.
In fact, you are so welcome that we made a sign to show you…

DIRECTIONS:

1. Cut each of the letters on the solid yellow lines. If you have one, use a ⅛" hole punch to punch the holes.

2. Weave twine through the holes as shown.

3. Tie loops at the ends of the twine so you can hang your sign.

4. Hang and enjoy! Welcome!

WHAT YOU NEED:

- Scissors
- Twine

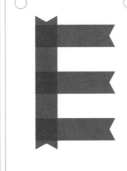

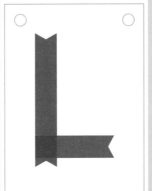

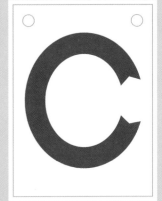

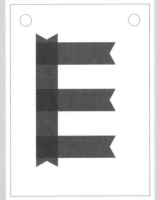

5

CUTIE HOUSE
COME IN! COME IN!

Put your feet up and get comfy. Your house is one of the cutest on the block!
His name is Cecil.

HOME SWEET HOME

WHAT YOU NEED:

- Scissors
- Double-sided tape
- Glue

Cut out all of the shapes on the solid yellow lines. Fold on all dotted yellow lines.

Take the main house and use double-sided tape on the large tab to secure. Stand upright.

Fold in the tabs on the top of the house. Use double-sided tape to attach the roof.

Construct the chimney. Fold in the bottom tabs. Apply a small amount of glue to the tabs. Center on the roof and press to secure.

You're ready to move in!!!

8

THE KIDS

We are going to be your new friends!

CAN YOU COME OUT AND PLAY?

We need a fifth friend for our group, and we think that you would be perfect!

LET'S PLAY

WHAT YOU NEED:

- Scissors
- Double-sided tape
- Glue

Cut out all of the shapes on the solid yellow lines. Fold on all dotted yellow lines.

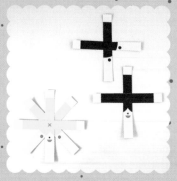

Take the head pieces and create two "+"s. Cross the "+"s as shown above to make a "*".

Fold over the center piece and secure it to the piece directly across from it using double-sided tape.

Move around the shape and attach each strip to the bottom center with tape. This will create a ball shape.

Roll the body into a tube and use double-sided tape on the large tab to secure.

Fold in the small tabs on the top of the body. Apply a small amount of glue on the tabs. Center on the head and press to secure.

Go outside and play, but don't stay out too late!

12

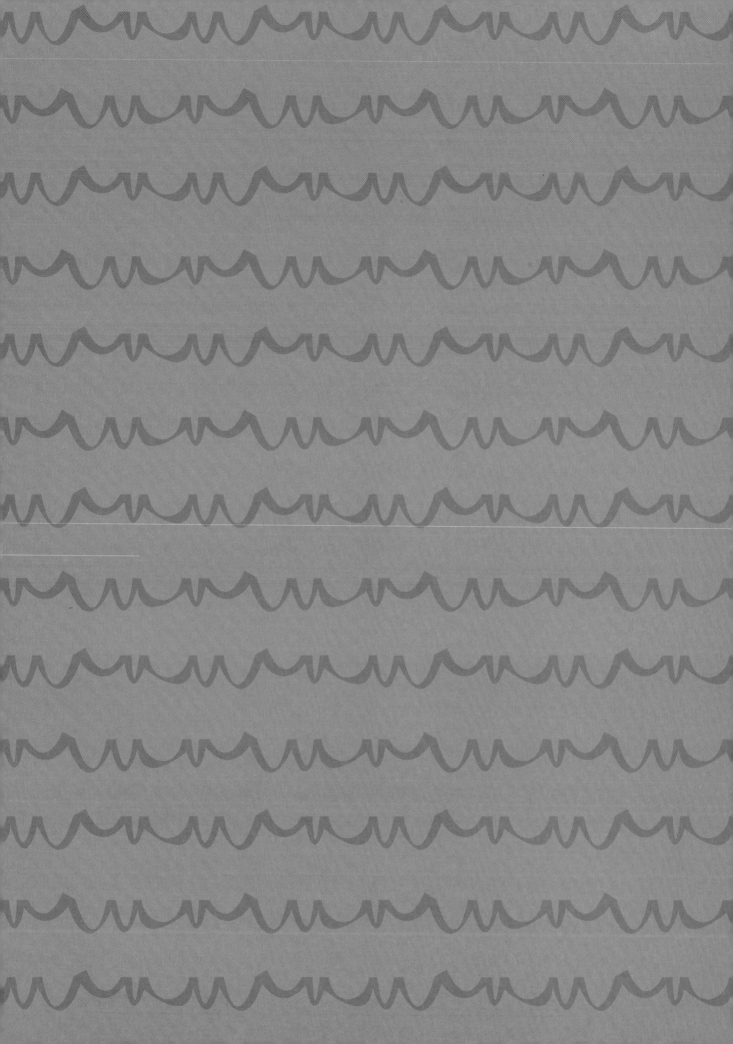

UMBRELLAS

OH NO!!!
It's pouring rain!

You better grab
your umbrella and
your galoshes!

RAINY

WHAT YOU NEED:

- Scissors
- Double-sided tape
- Pipe cleaners

Cut out all of the shapes on the solid yellow lines. Fold on all dotted yellow lines.

Take the umbrella and use double-sided tape on the large tab to secure.

Cut a pipe cleaner to about 2½" and insert into the top hole of the umbrella.

Loop over the top of the pipe cleaner and re-insert the tip into the hole. Bend the bottom into a "J."

Don't forget your jacket!

TERU TERU BOZU

A teru teru bozu is a little charm you make when it rains. It is supposed to have magical powers to make the rain go away!

He is an easy friend to make—here's how:

1. Ball up half a sheet of paper.

2. Wrap another full sheet of paper around the ball and tie a string around its "neck"—it should look like a ghost! Draw on a little face.

3. Hang in the window and wish for sunny days!

TOASTER TIME

It's breakfast time!

We'll make the eggs. You make the toast…

RISE AND SHINE

WHAT YOU NEED:

- Scissors
- Double-sided tape

Cut out all the shapes on the solid blue lines. Fold on all dotted blue lines.

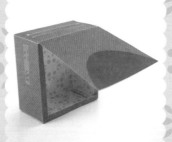

Construct the main part of the toaster. Leave the large back panel open so that you can add all of the inside parts.

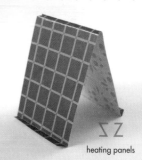

heating panels

Take the two heating panels and fold them into a "Z" formation. The top tabs should fold in toward each other. Use doubled-sided tape to attach them together.

Use double-sided tape and attach the top of the heating panels to the inside top center panel of the toaster between the bread slots.

Fold the tabs on the lever up.

Slide the lever over the heating panels. Use double-sided tape to affix the bottom of the heating panels to the bottom of the toaster. The lever handles should fit through the side openings of the toaster.

Close the back of the toaster.

Move the lever up and down to make the toast pop out!

Breakfast is served!

CAMERA ADVENTURE

Getting bored in the neighborhood?

It's nice and all, but let's go
do something exciting!
Let's go on an adventure!
It doesn't matter where!
Grab your camera and let's go!

FLASH, SNAP, CLICK, CLICK...

WHAT YOU NEED:

- Scissors
- Double-sided tape
- Glue

Cut out all the shapes on the solid blue lines. Fold on all dotted blue lines.

Construct the main part of the camera, but leave the back open so that you can fit your pictures inside.

lens

rewind crank   shutter button

Roll the lens, shutter button and rewind crank into tubes. Use double-sided tape on the tabs to secure.

shutter button   rewind crank

Insert the shutter button into the "X" on the top left of the camera. Insert the rewind crank into the "X" on the top right of the camera.

Fold in the small tabs on the camera lens and apply a small amount of glue to the tabs and the rim. Center the lens over the lens area on the front of the camera.

Construct the view finder and use double-sided tape to attach it to the top center of the main camera.

Roll the flash into a cone. Use double-sided tape on the tab to secure. Roll the flash attacher into a tube and glue the tab to the back of the flash.

Insert the flash attacher into the top of the "X" on the top of the viewfinder.

Make the strap into a loop and slide it into the side panel; secure it with glue inside of the camera. Place the pictures inside of the back of the camera and shut the back panel.

You're ready to travel the world!

click

24

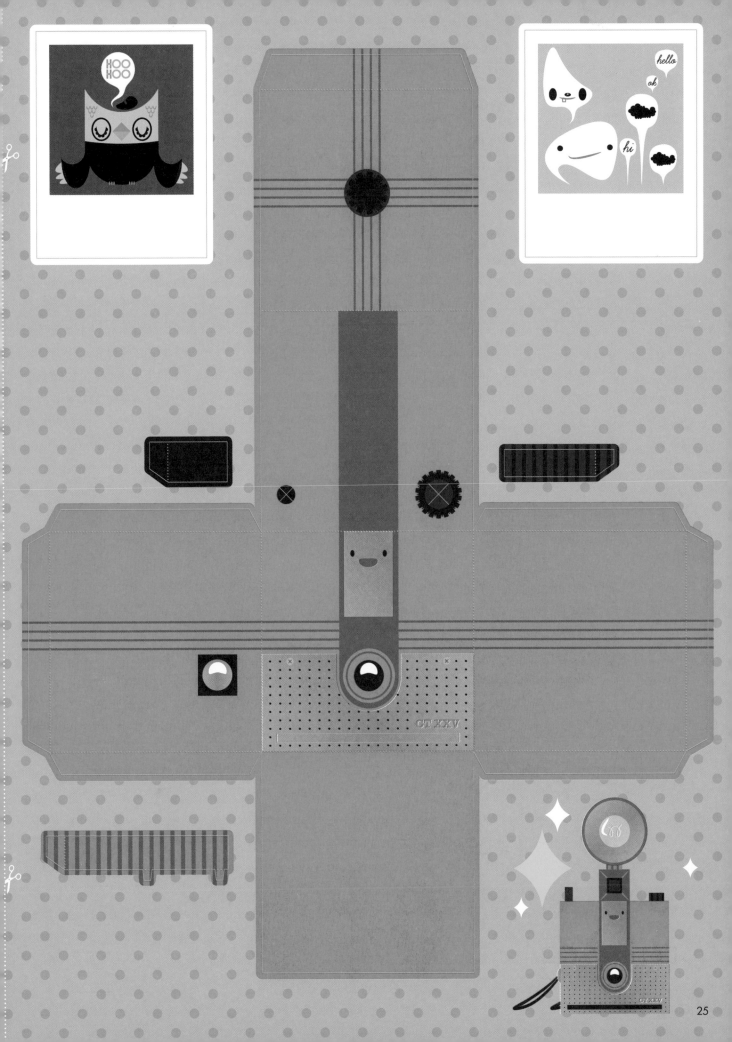

MAKE
YOUR OWN
PHOTOS
v ‿ v

MAKE
YOUR OWN
PHOTOS
v ‿ v

MAKE
YOUR OWN
PHOTOS
v ‿ v

Cut out the center square of the photo frame. Glue your own picture to the back so it shows through the frame.

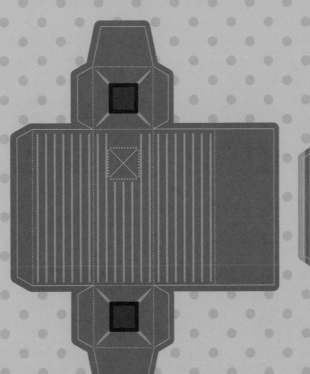

THE FOREST

The forest is just the first stop on our adventure! Let's climb trees and go on a hike.
We are going to befriend all the animals and go searching for gnomes. Who knows what we'll find!

TREES AND MUSHROOMS

PLANT YOURSELF AND STAY AWHILE...

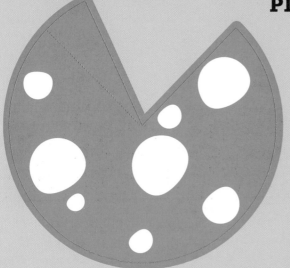

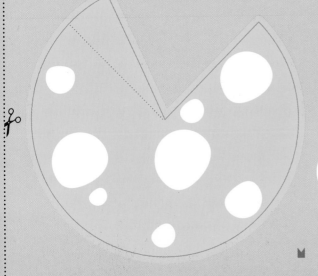

WHAT YOU NEED:

- Scissors
- Double-sided tape
- Glue

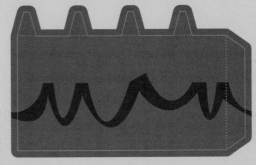

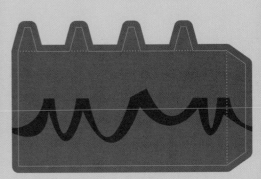

Pull up a toadstool and have a seat! The gnomes and trees are here to greet you and tell you stories about all the forest creatures.

DIRECTIONS:

1. Cut out all of the shapes on the solid yellow lines. Fold on all dotted yellow lines.

2. Roll the stem into a tube and use double sided tape on the large tab to secure.

3. Roll the mushroom into a small cone and use double-sided tape on the large tab to secure.

4. Fold out the small tabs on the top of the stem. Apply a small amount of glue to the inside of each tab and connect the bottom of the mushroom.

5. Time to frolic and hang out with the gnomes!

MR. GNOME

Who is that little man hiding in the bushes???

GNOME AWAY FROM HOME

WHAT YOU NEED:

- Scissors
- Double-sided tape
- Twine

Cut out all the shapes on the solid white and yellow lines. Fold on all dotted white and yellow lines.

Construct the head of the gnome into a box.

Construct the body. Fold the inner legs up—the tabs should connect to each other.

Leave the top of the body open.

Construct the arms.

Knot a piece of twine on one end and pull it through the left arm. Run the twine through the body and then through the right arm. Knot again on the outside of the right arm.

Close the top of the body. Using double-sided tape, attach the head to the body.

Roll the hat into a cone and put it on top of the gnome's head.

He's ready to tell you stories and make you a sandwich!

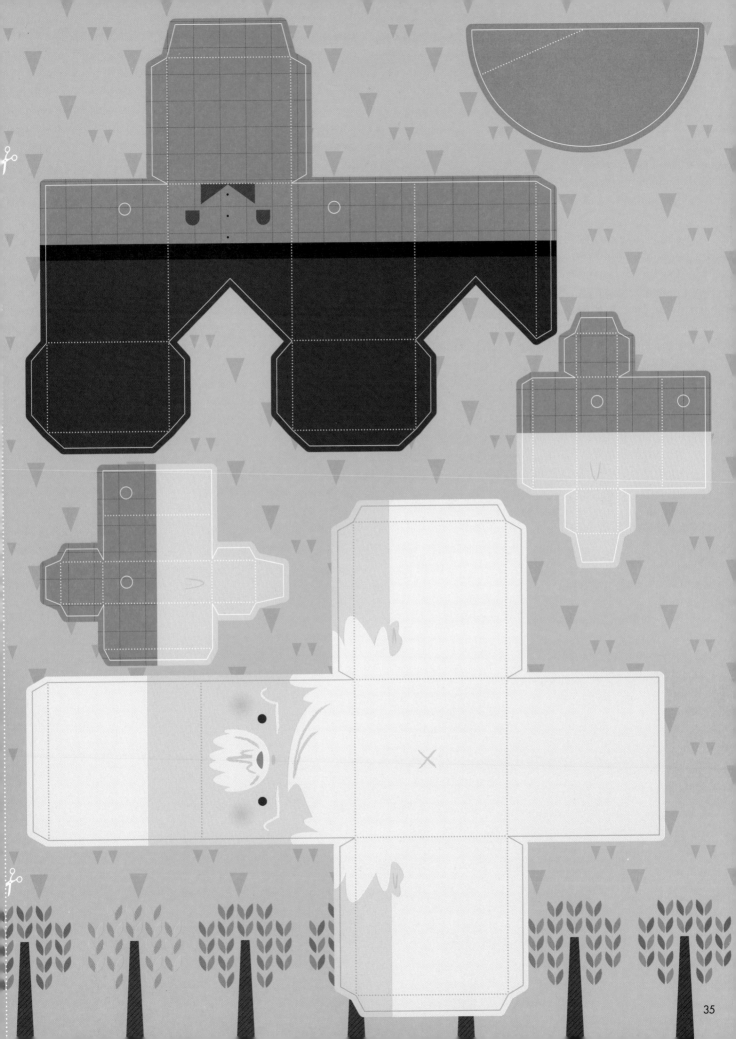

APPLE MOBILE

The sandwiches the gnomes made were great, but I'm still hungry. Maybe we can reach some of those apples in that tree…

AN APPLE A DAY...

WHAT YOU NEED:

- Scissors
- Double-sided tape
- Twine

Cut out all the shapes on the solid white lines. Fold on all dotted white lines.

Roll the tree into a tube and use double-sided tape on the large tab to secure.

Loop the twine around the tree. Knot about 3" from the top of the tube. Tie the straps together and make a loop so that you can hang it later!

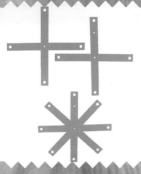

Take the apple pieces and create two "+"s - Cross the "+"s as shown above to make a "*".

Fold over the center piece and secure it to the piece directly across from it using double-sided tape.

Move around the shape and attach each strip to the bottom center with tape. This will create a ball shape.

Roll the apple stem into a tube and insert it into the top of the apple.

Use double-sided tape and place the leaves on the apple near the stem.

Pull Through!

Knot

Use a long piece of twine and knot it on one end. Pull it through the apple and through the stem.

Tie an apple to each strap on the tree. Pull the twine through the center hole on the tree to attach the third apple.

Time for a sweet treat!

38

GRRR! BEAR

Oh no, a bear! I hope he's friendly... and likes apples.

RAAWWRRRRR!!!

WHAT YOU NEED:

- Scissors
- Double-sided tape

Cut out all of the shapes on the solid yellow lines. Fold on all dotted yellow lines.

Fold the main body of the bear. Bend the long top panel across the top. Use double-sided tape on the tabs to attach.

Fold up the bottom panel and use doubled-sided tape on the large tab to complete the body.

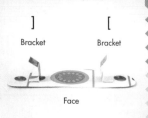

]
Bracket

[
Bracket

Face

Fold the face attachments into brackets. Use double-sided tape on the brackets to attach the additional face piece. Now the muzzle is 3-D!

Use douple-sided tape on the ears and place.

Use double-_____ tape o_ ___ tail ___ and place.

_____ place near the _____ place to hide.

He is ready to nap and eat!

44

OWLBERT

Hoo Hoo! Who goes there? Is that you, Owlbert?
Do you think we can stay in your tree for awhile?

HOO HOO! HOO HOO!

WHAT YOU NEED:

- Scissors
- Double-sided tape

Cut out all the shapes on the solid gray lines. Fold on all dotted gray lines.

Fold the main body, use double-sided tape on the large tab to secure.

Fold the feet into rectangles. Make sure not to forget to cut the slots in the side!

Place the owl upright and slide the front and back into the slots on the side of the feet.

Start by folding the wings on the center line, then bend the sides up to meet the center and create a tear drop shape. Use double-sided tape to secure.

Using double-sided tape, secure the wings to the side of the body.

Owlbert is ready to take flight!!

VEST BUNNY

Where did you get that vest, bunny?
Did you make it yourself?
Or did you steal it, just like you are going
to steal those carrots?!

VEST BUNNY

WHAT YOU NEED:

- Scissors
- Double-sided tape

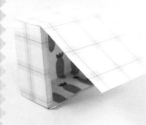

Cut out all the shapes on the solid gray and white lines. Fold on all dotted gray and white lines.

Construct the body of the bunny. Leave the large back panel open so that you can add the ears and arms.

Slide the arms into the front slots and tape inside for reinforcement.

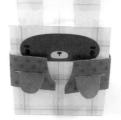

Slide the ears into the top slots and tape inside for reinforcement.

Close the back of the body to complete the bunny.

Wrap the vest around the bunny to keep him warm. Slide his arms through the vest slots.

He is ready to go and play in his carrot garden!

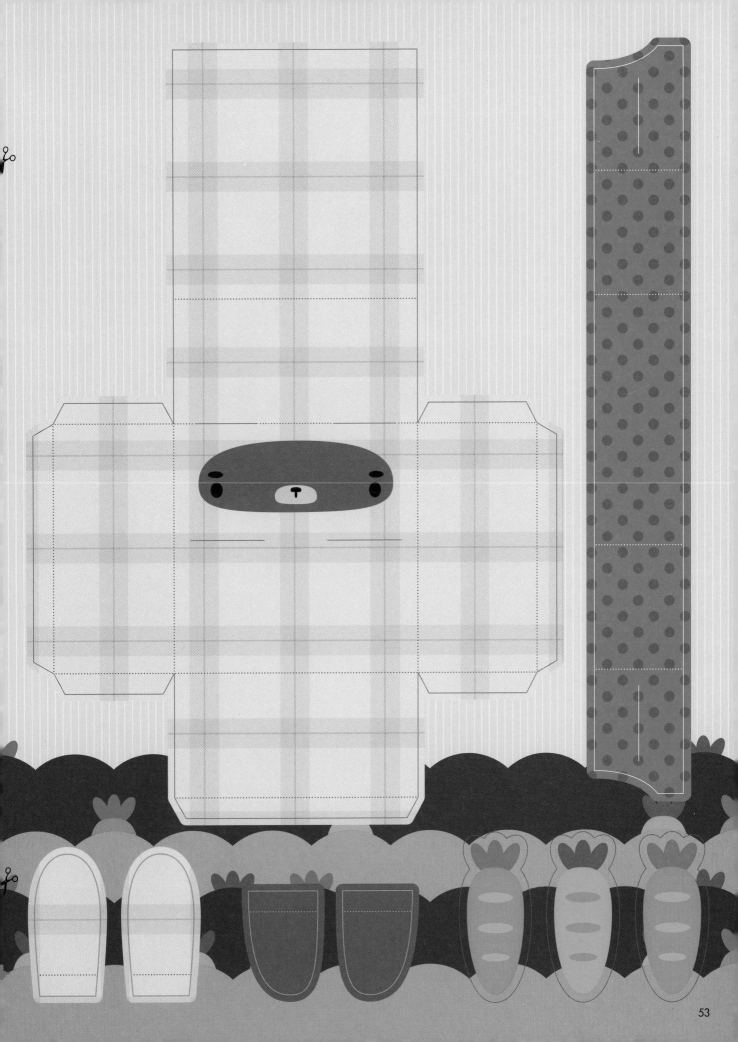

MUSTACHES

We've been in the forest so long, we've grown crazy mustaches!

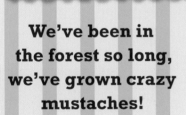

55

WHAT'S ON YOUR FACE?

WHAT YOU NEED:

- Scissors
- Double-sided tape

Cut out all of the shapes on the solid gray and brown lines.

Use the "Super Fun Comb" to groom your favorite mustache.

Stick double-sided tape to the back of your favorite mustache and put it on your upper lip.

Time to show off your face to your friends and family!

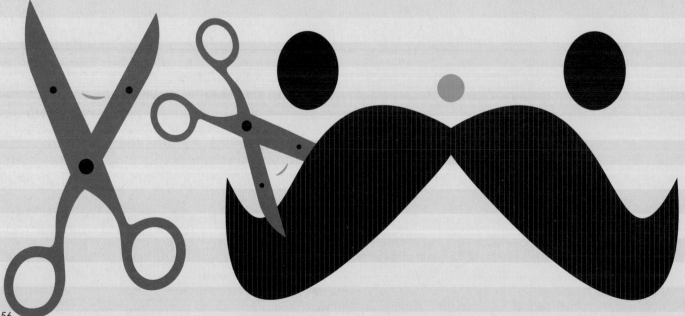

Super Fun Comb

57

THE OCEAN

THE OCEAN

It's too bad we have to take this spooky ship to travel across the ocean. I think it might be haunted! We'll make the best of it, though, if we stick together!

PIRATE GHOST

Don't be afraid! The Pirate Ghost is our friend. He is here to guide us to the treasure! Yarg!

DIRECTIONS:

1. Cut out all of the shapes on the solid yellow lines. Fold on all dotted yellow lines.

2. Fold the ghost in half, use double-sided tape on the large tab to secure.

3. Bend the "V" so that the edge of the paper without the tab overlaps and lines up with the dotted line. The top tab should be sticking straight up. The top of the head should be slightly domed. Repeat on the back side.

4. Fold the pirate hat in half, use double sided tape on the large tab to secure.

5. Use double-sided tape to secure the hat to the tabs on the ghost's head.

6. Time to go treasure hunting! Yarg!

WHAT YOU NEED:

- Scissors
- Double-sided tape

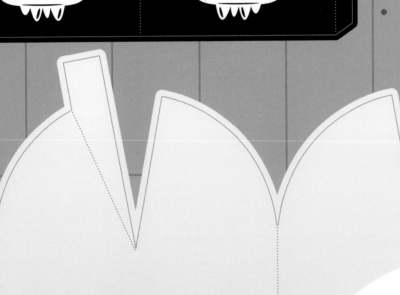

61

WHALE

Is that a whale in the distance?

Maybe he can give us a ride to the next island!

SPLISH! SPLASH!

WHAT YOU NEED:

- Scissors
- Double-sided tape
- Pipe cleaners

Cut out all the shapes on the solid blue and white lines. Fold on all dotted blue and white lines.

Fold the whale in half. Use double-sided tape on the large tab to secure.

Bend the "V" and overlap the front of the face so that it lines up with the dotted line. The top of the head should be slightly domed. Repeat on the back side.

Fold the fins out. Push in the body on the sides to make it slightly more rounded.

Fold the undersisde of the tail up to meet the top of the tail. Curl the tail up. Use double-sided tape on the inside to secure.

Curl pipe cleaners around your finger to create curly water.

Insert the pipe cleaners into the blowhole.

Roll the water piece into a tube. Use double-sided tape on the large tab to secure. Place the whale on top.

Time for a swim!

64

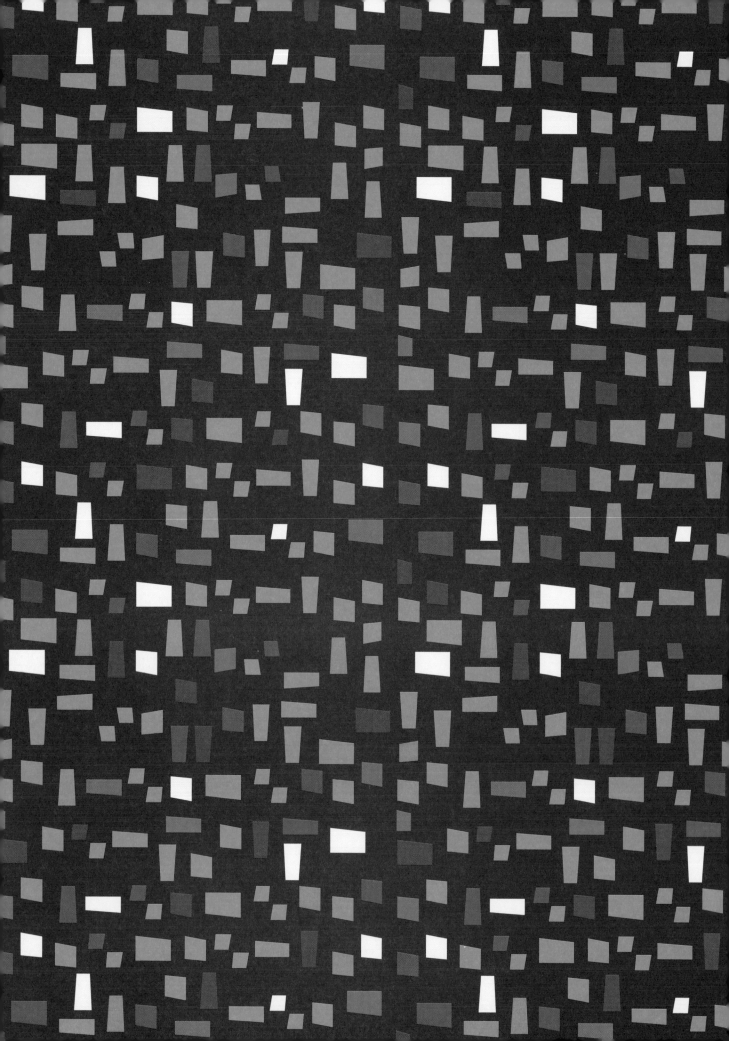

OCTOPUS

He's got his headband on.
(I think that means it's time to party!)

8-ARMED PARTY

WHAT YOU NEED:

- Scissors
- Double-sided tape
- Pencil
- Glue

Cut out all of the shapes on the solid purple lines except for the inner leg lines. Those are for later. Fold on all dotted purple lines.

Fold the octopus in half on the center line. Glue the entire body together. After the glue dries, cut on the leg lines.

Fold the body in half again. Use double-sided tape on the large tab to secure.

Use a pencil to roll up the legs.

Set the octopus upright. Push in the body on the sides to make it slightly more rounded.

Tie the headband around his head.

Time for that 8-armed hug!

HUG?

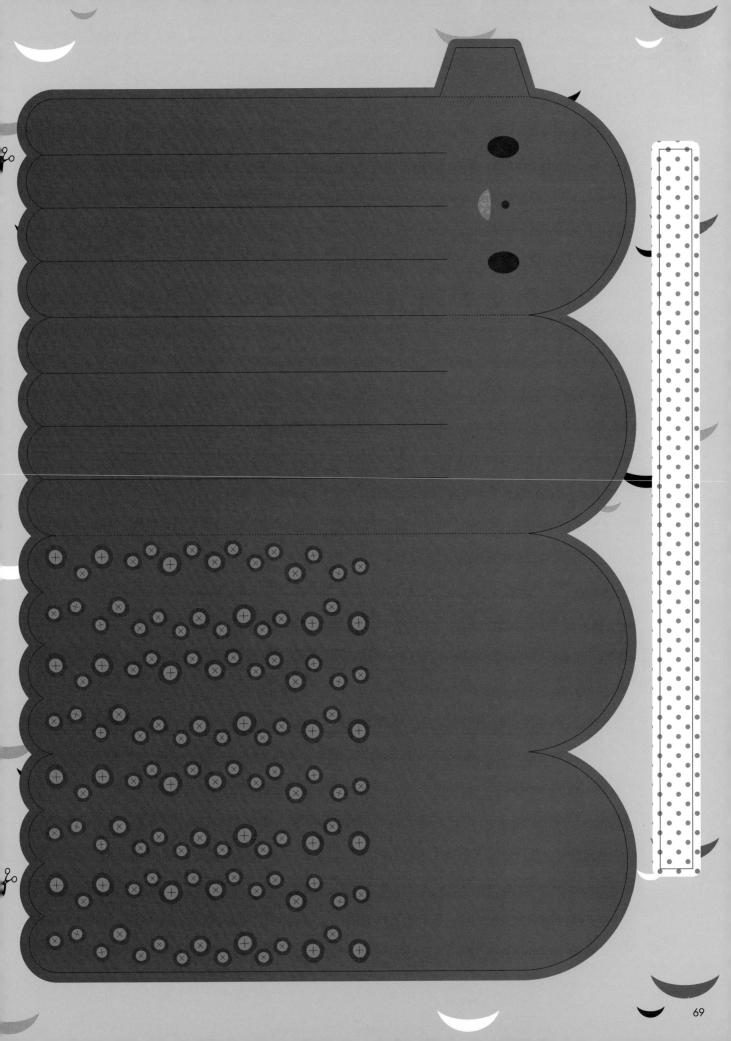

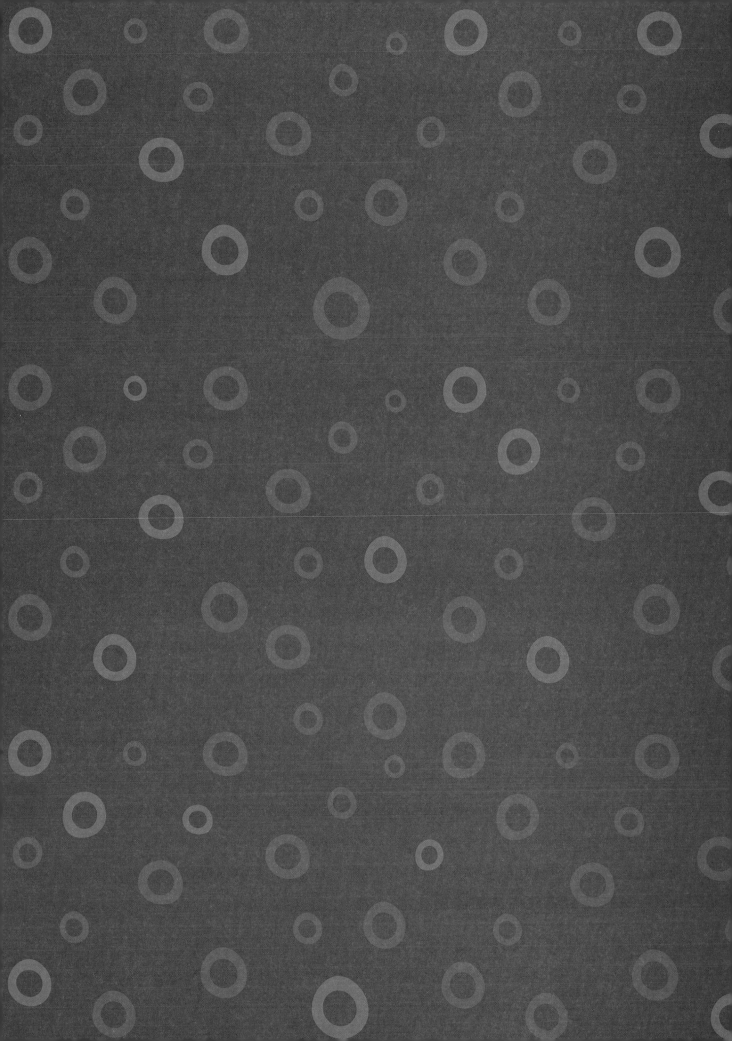

PLAID TURTLE

Aw, little turtle.
We are looking for treasure!

Do you think you can help?
Hurry! Hurry!

TREASURE TURTLE

WHAT YOU NEED:

- Scissors
- Double-sided tape

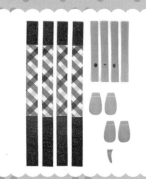

Cut out all the shapes on the solid white lines. Fold on all dotted white lines.

Take the head pieces and create two "+"s. Cross the "+"s as shown above to make a "*".

Move around the shape and attach each strip to the bottom center with tape. This will create a ball shape. Put the head aside for now.

Create the shell by creating two "+"s. Cross the "+"s to make a "*". Use the plaid section to center it.

tape here

Apply double-sided tape to the short tab. Bend the shell to make a dome. Place the short tab inside the long tab. Move around the circle until the shell is completed.

Use small pieces of tape between the layers of the shell to reinforce.

Turn the shell upright.

Attach double-sided tape to the back of the head and attach it to the body.

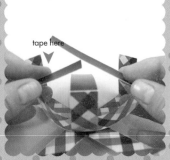

Turn the turtle on his shell and attach the feet and tail to the underside.

Turn him right side up. Whew! Much better. Fold the legs and tail down.

I think he's ready to lead you to the treasure!

TREASURE BOX!

FINALLY!
We found it!
We're rich!

TREASURE!

WHAT YOU NEED:

- Scissors
- Double-sided tape

Cut out all of the shapes on the solid yellow lines. Fold on all dotted yellow lines.

Construct the lid of the treasure chest.

Construct the bottom portion of the treasure chest. Fold out the back hinge.

Attach the lid to the back hinge using double-sided tape.

Attach the top lock piece to the inside center of the lid.

Pull a piece of twine through the holes to build the lock.

Fill the box with treasure!!!

Close the lid and pull the twine through the top lock. Tie the twine into a bow.

Draw your own map to locate your treasure!

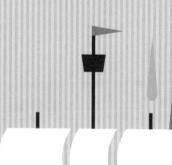

Hide the map from your enemies! Time to go on the hunt!

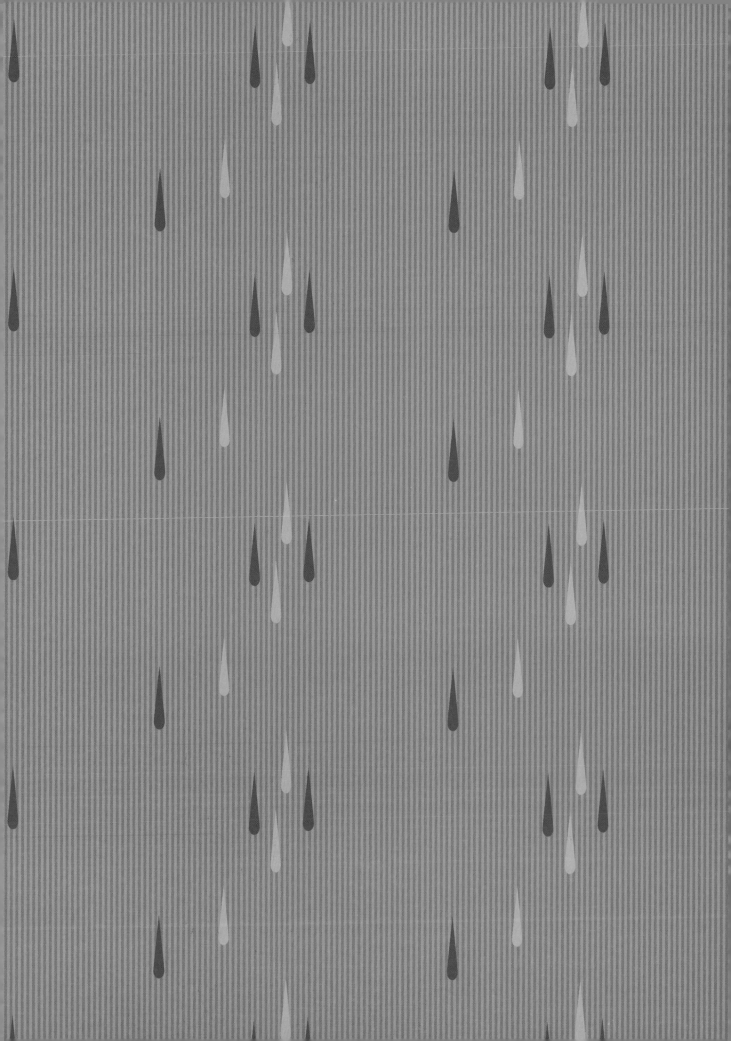

HERMIT CRAB

More like SNEAKY CRAB!

We see all those treasures under your shell.

YOU AREN'T GETTING OURS!

HERMIT CRAB

WHAT YOU NEED:

- Scissors
- Double-sided tape

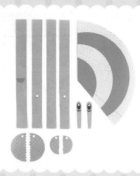

Cut out all the shapes on the solid gray lines. Fold on all dotted gray lines.

Take the head pieces and create two "+"s. Cross the "+"s as shown above to make a "*".

Cut two 3" pieces of string. Tie a knot on one end of the string and pull one through each hole.

Pull the string through the claw pieces and tie a small knot to secure them to the body. Cut off excess string.

Fold over the center piece and secure it to the piece directly across from it using double-sided tape.

Move around the shape and attach each strip to the bottom center with tape. This will create a ball shape.

Use double-sided tape on the eyes and place.

Roll the shell into a cone.

Apply a small amount of glue to the inside of the cone and slide it over the back of the body.

Watch out! He is going to pinch you!

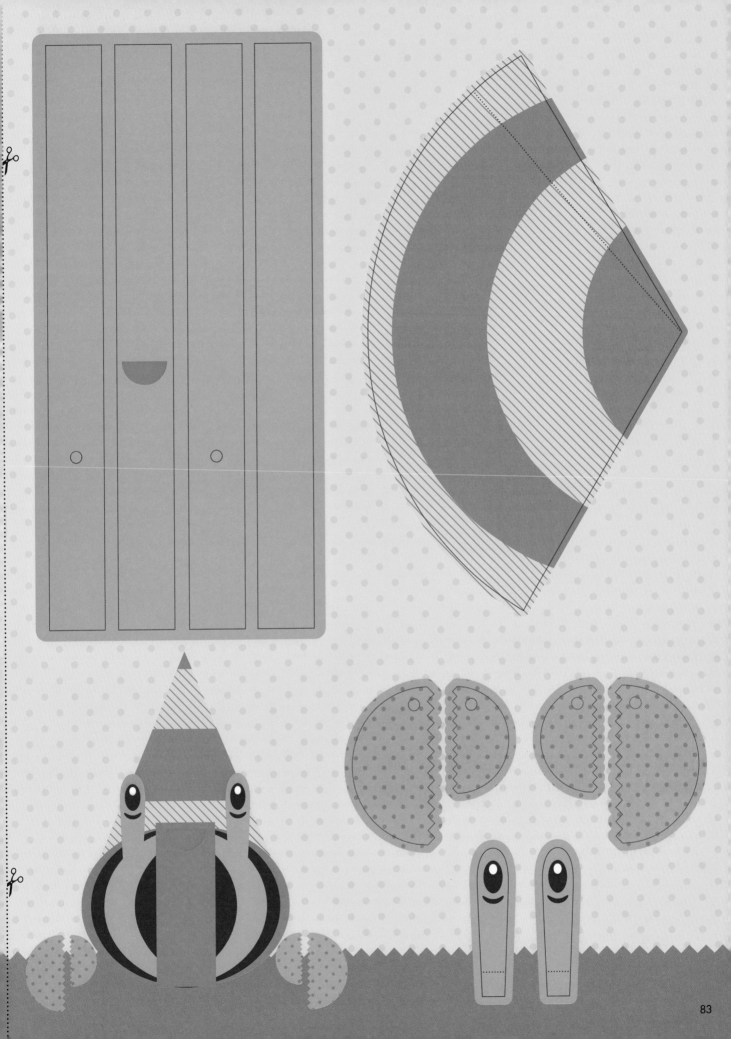

PARACHUTE NOTE

I think I'm getting seasick.
I found a helicopter to get off of the island.
Let's grab our treasure and go!
We can parachute to safety!

WHAT YOU NEED:

- Scissors
- Double-sided tape

Cut out all the shapes on the solid white lines. Fold on all dotted white lines.

Construct the monster box!

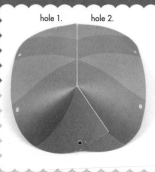

hole 1.   hole 2.

Overlap the sides so that hole 1 and hole 2 are lined up over each other. Use double-sided tape to secure. This should create a dome shape. Repeat on the other side.

Cut six pieces of twine that are 5" long.

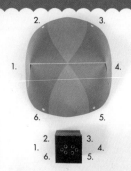

The holes around the edge of the parachute correspond with the holes on the top the box. Make a note of the numbers above.

Knot a piece of twine at one end and pull it through a hole on the parachute. Repeat for all holes.

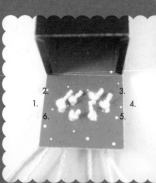

Pull the corresponding parachute twine through the hole on the box. Tie a knot to secure the twine to the box.

Write a special note and put it inside the box.

Drop the parachute on your unexpecting recipient!

You've landed safely and delivered your message! Hooray!

THE JUNGLE

THE JUNGLE

Woo hoo! Wheee! Parachuting into the jungle was a lot of fun.
Let's swing through the trees and hug the monkeys! Everywhere we go, we have the best time!

LEAFY FAN

Whoo! It sure is hot in the jungle. We should use those leaves and make a fan!

WHAT YOU NEED:

- Scissors
- Twine

DIRECTIONS:

1. Cut out the shape on the solid gray lines.

2. Fold on the dotted lines. Fold back and forth as if it were an accordian.

3. After folding, flatten and run a piece of twine through the hole on bottom. Tie a knot and a bow. The top should fan out.

4. Now we can stay cool and relax. Make multiple fans and hang them as a banner!

ELEPHANT

Aww, what a sweet lady! This elephant wants to give us a ride to our next destination!

ELE-FUN

WHAT YOU NEED:

- Scissors
- Double-sided tape
- Twine

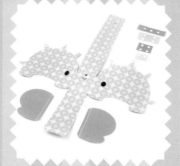

Cut out all the shapes on the solid white lines. Fold on all dotted white lines.

Take the trunk piece that has three holes and pull a 2" piece of twine through the center hole.

Roll the trunk pieces into tubes.

Insert tube 2 into tube 1. Line up the holes in tube 1 with the top holes in tube 2. Pull twine through the holes and knot on each side. Repeat with tubes 2 and 3, and 3 and 4.

The trunk willl look like the piece above when completed. Attach the trunk to the elephant by pulling twine through the small hole above her mouth. Tie a knot on the inside to secure.

Fold the main body of the elephant. Bend the long top panel across the top. Use double-sided tape on the tabs to attach.

Before closing the bottom, make sure to pull a piece of twine through the back to create the tail.

Close the bottom panel and stand the elephant upright.

Attach the ears to the side of the head using double-sided tape on the large tabs.

She wants to give you a ride! Let's go!

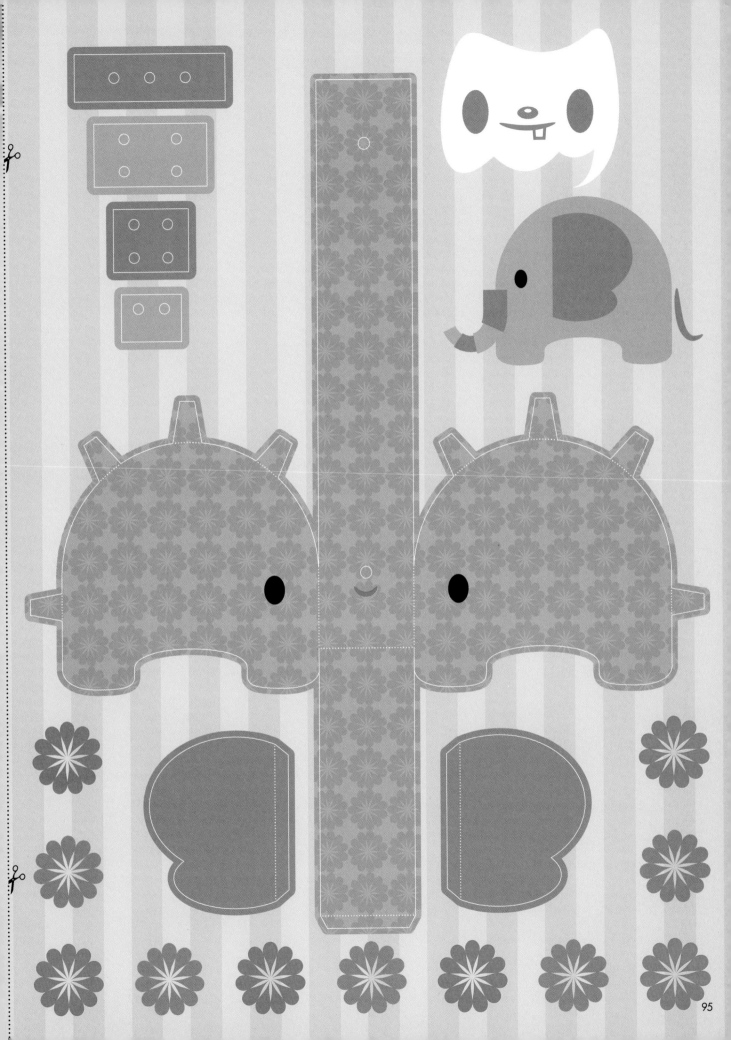

MONKEY

Ooo! Ooo! Ooo!
Eee! Eee! Eee!
It's time for us to swing
through the trees!

MONKEY SEE! MONKEY DO!

WHAT YOU NEED:

- Scissors
- Double-sided tape
- Twine

Cut out all the shapes on the solid white lines. Fold on all dotted white lines.

Take the largest strips and create two "+"s. Cross the "+"s as shown above to make a "*". This will make the head.

Move around the shape and attach each strip to the bottom center with tape. This will create a ball shape.

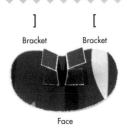

Fold the face attachments into brackets. Use double-sided tape on the brackets to attach the additional face piece. Now the face is 3-D!

Use double-sided tape on the ears and place on head.

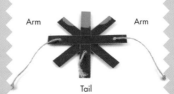

Take the body pieces and create two "+"s. Cross the "+"s as shown above to make a "*". Pull twine through the three holes.

Move around the shape and attach each strip to the bottom center with tape. This will create a ball shape.

Create a 90-degree angle using two of the medium-sized leg pieces. Take the bottom strip and fold it across the top strip. Repeat this step until the leg is an accordian piece and you can't fold it over any more. Repeat to construct the second leg.

When the legs are completed, they should look like the ones above. Use double-sided tape to attach the feet.

Place the head on top of the body and place the legs at the front of the body. Attach using double-sided tape.

We are ready to swing through the trees!

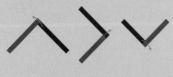

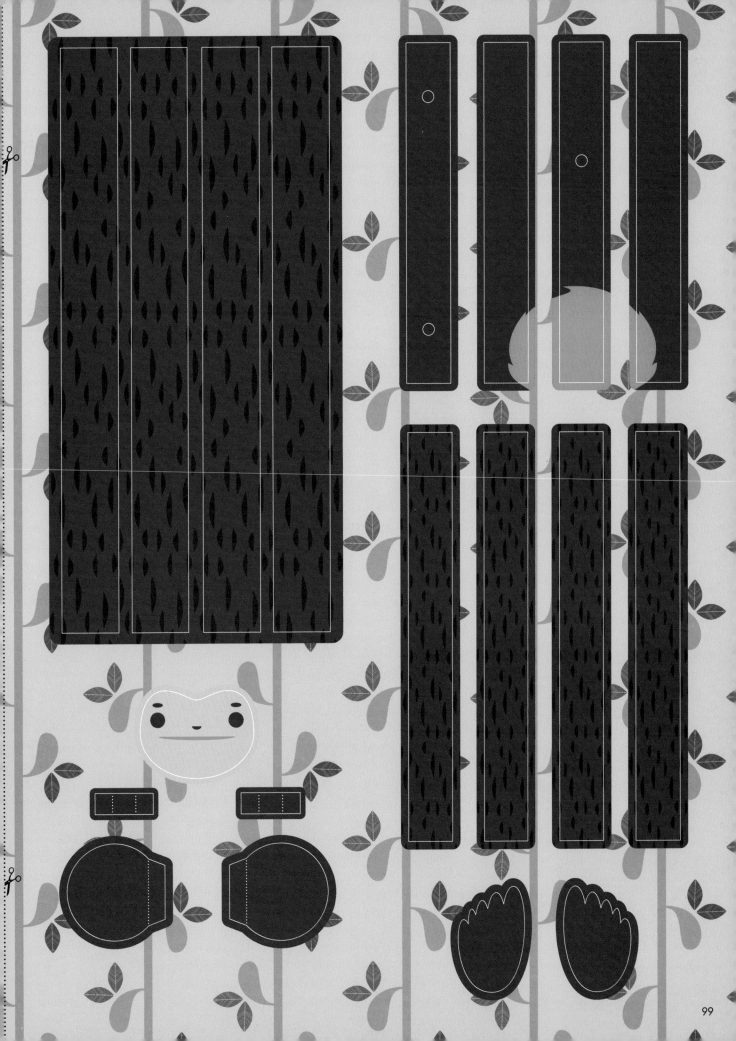

ALLIGATOR
CHOMP! BITE! SNAP! OH MY!

SEE YA LATER

WHAT YOU NEED:

• Scissors

Cut out all the shapes on the solid yellow lines. Fold on all dotted yellow lines.

Begin by folding the legs down.

Fold on the center line and fold the tail so it points up!

After the body is folded in half, fold left and right on the diagonal lines across the head.

Push down at the point where all of the folds meet on the head. The mouth will pop open!

Fold down the teeth so they are extra scary!

The alligator is ready to bite and chomp!

GROWL!!! GROWL!!!

WHAT YOU NEED:

- Scissors
- Double-sided tape
- Pipe cleaners

Cut out all the shapes on the solid yellow lines. Fold on all dotted yellow lines.

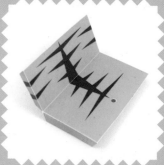

Fold the body into a box. Use double-sided tape on the large tabs to secure.

Fold the back piece as shown above.

Attach the back piece to the back of the body box using double-sided tape.

Attach the back legs to the back bottom corners.

Attach the face to the front of the body box using double-sided tape.

Curl a pipe cleaner around your finger to create the tail.

Insert the tail into the hole in the back.

Growl! Growl! Growl!

106

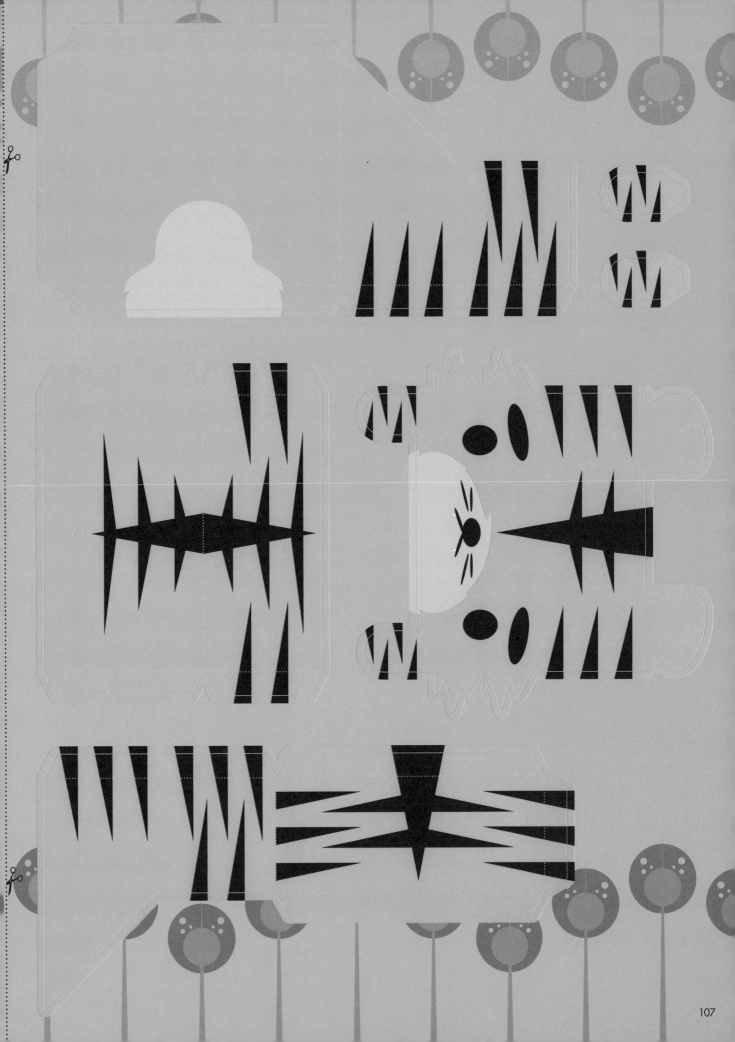

GIRAFFE

What are you doing in the jungle?
You don't live here! You're here on vacation?
Let's share our pictures!

GIRAFFE ON VACATION

WHAT YOU NEED:

- Scissors
- Double-sided tape
- Twine
- Glue

Cut out all the shapes on the solid gray lines. Fold on all dotted gray lines.

Construct the main body. Don't forget to pull a small piece of twine through the hole to create the tail.

Fold the the two flaps on the face up as shown. Using glue, attach the antennae to the inside of the head, facing out.

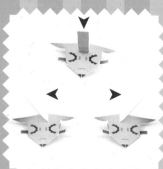

Turn the head over. Fold the neck piece forward, left, then right.

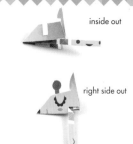

inside out

right side out

Fold the head in half so it is inside out. Then, fold just the face and antennae right side out. Because of the folds you made in the last step, the neck piece should face down.

Construct the neck.

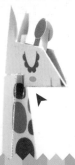

Slide the head into the top of the neck. Make sure that the head fits into the notch cut on the front of the neck so that it doesn't fall off!

glue here

Slide the head and neck into place. Use double-sided tape on the large front tab to secure. Add a small drop of glue behind the neck to hold it to the body.

Construct the legs.

Glue the legs to each of the bottom corners of the body.

From way up there, you must have the best view!

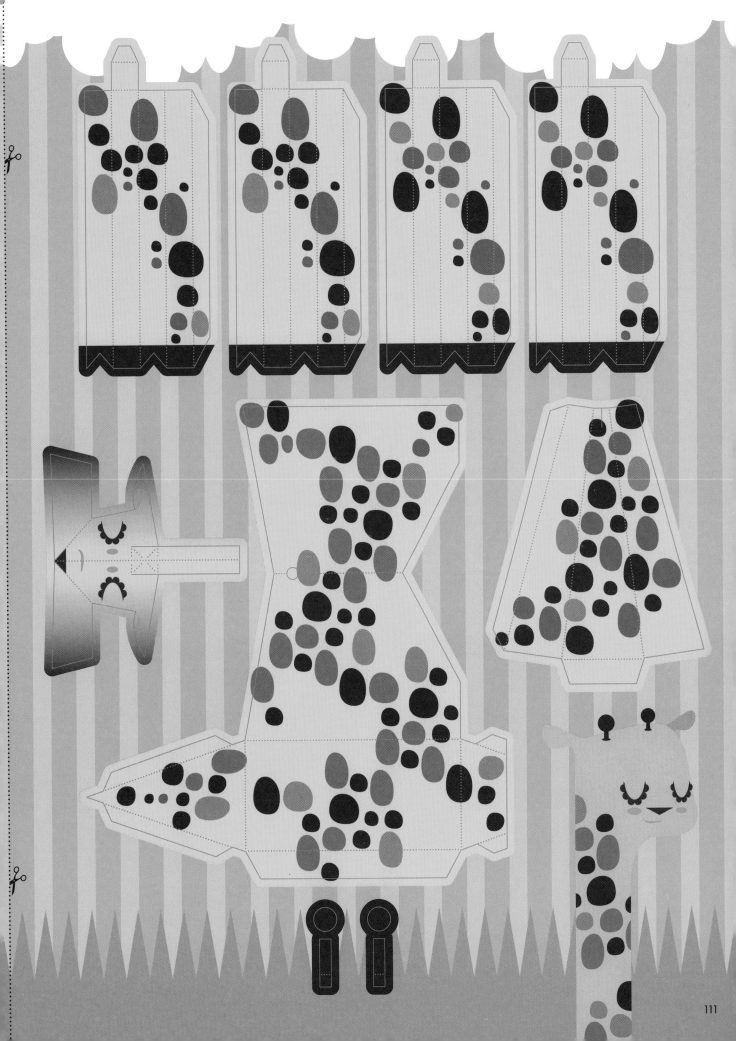

111

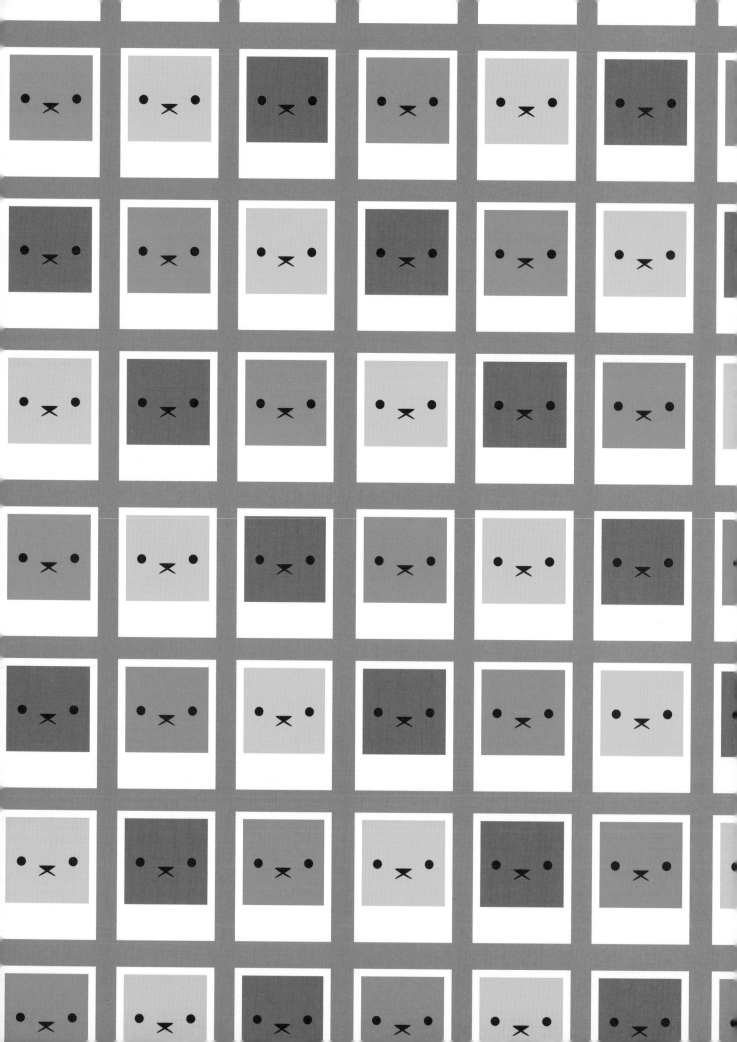

AIRPLANE

I think our adventure is almost over.
Let's head back to the city and get something to eat!

TIME FOR TAKEOFF

WHAT YOU NEED:

• Scissors

Cut out the shape on the solid yellow line.

Begin by folding the plane in half.

Fold the top corners to the center.

Fold the body in half again with the top corners folded in.

Fold on the diagonal line. Turn over and repeat on the opposite side.

Fold on the rear wing line. Turn over and repeat on the opposite side.

We're ready for takeoff!

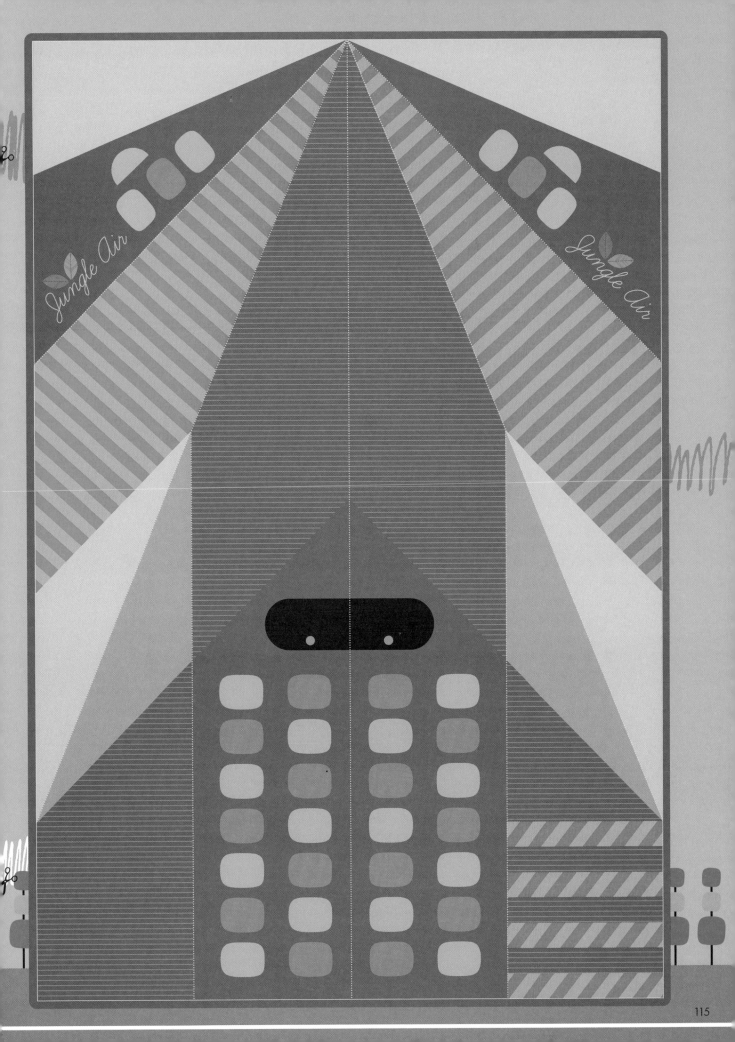

THE CITY

THE CITY

Wow! The big city. It's so amazing here! The buildings are huge, and there are so many people. This might be the end of our journey. I think I'm going settle down here for awhile.

YUMMY BURGER

WHAT YOU NEED:

- Scissors
- Double-sided tape
- Glue

DIRECTIONS:

1. Cut out the shapes on the solid white and red lines. Fold on the dotted white and red lines.

2. Build the patty by making a circle out of the long brown piece. Apply a small amount of glue on the tabs. Press the round patties to the top and bottom to secure.

3. Build the top bun by creating 2 "+"s. Cross the "+"s to make a "*". Apply double-sided tape to the short tab. Bend the bun to make a dome. Place the short tab inside the long tab. Move around the circle until the bun is completed. Repeat to create the bottom bun.

Place Tape Here

Line Up the Edge

4. Stack the burger in the order you like.

5. Yum yum! Eat up!

SKYLINE

**The buildings are lit up so pretty!
Does that one have
a message for you?**

SPECIAL MESSAGE!

WHAT YOU NEED:

- Scissors
- Double-sided tape
- Twine

Cut out all of the shapes on the solid white lines. Fold on all dotted white lines. Don't forget to cut out the windows!

Attach the support to the back side below the windows of the cityscape.

Fold up the back support and attach it to the side tabs on the city. This will create a pocket.

Attach the stand below the pocket and place the city upright.

Write a message in the windows! Use the chart below for reference or create your own letters.

Slide the window sign into the back pocket.

I think the city is trying to tell you something!

122

VROOM! VROOM!

This car is so zippy, it can
take us anywhere we need to go!

LET'S GO FOR A DRIVE!

WHAT YOU NEED:

- Scissors
- Double-sided tape
- Glue

Cut out all the shapes on the solid white and red lines. Fold on all dotted white and red lines.

Fold the main body of the car. Bend the long top panel across the top. Use double-sided tape on the tabs to attach.

Fold up the bottom panel and use double-sided tape on the large tab to complete the body.

Bend the fenders in the middle to create a dome. Use double-sided tape to secure.

Glue the fenders to the front and back of the car.

Roll the axles into tubes. Use double-sided tape to secure.

Push the axles through the holes in body of the car.

Put the tires over the axles. Repeat on the the opposite side.

Glue the wheel covers to the tabs on the axles. Repeat on the opposite side.

Personalize the license plate and attach to the back using double-sided tape.

Vroom! Vroom! Let's go! Let's go!

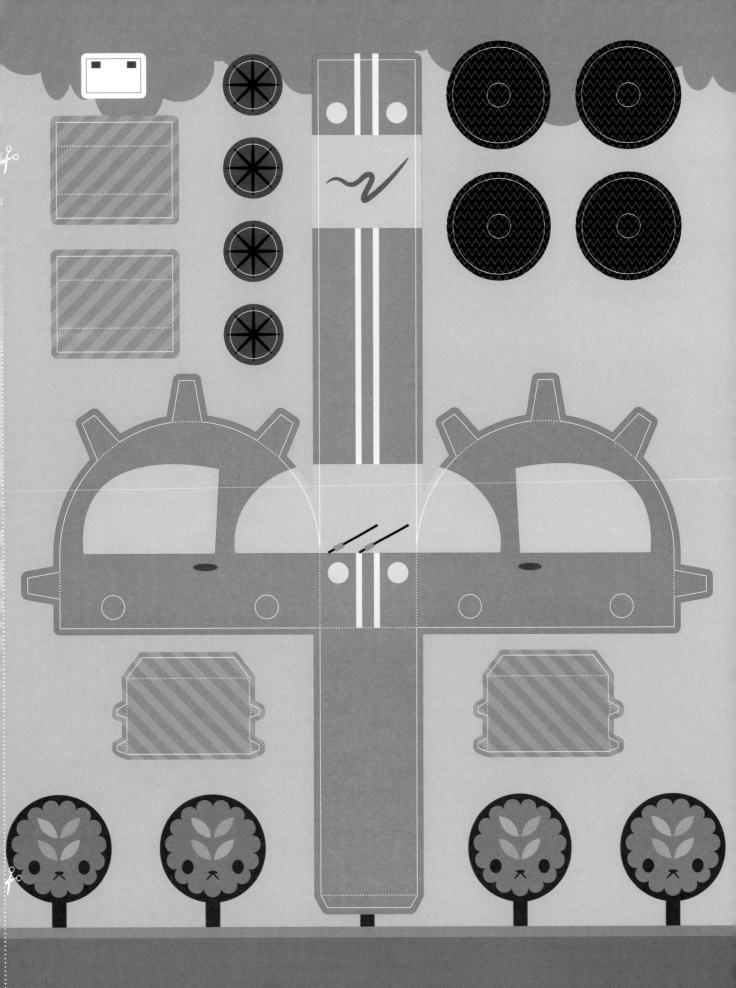

ZZZ...ZZZ...ZZZ...

WHAT YOU NEED:

- Scissors
- Double-sided tape
- Glue

Cut out all of the shapes on the solid red and blue lines. Fold on all dotted red and blue lines.

Construct the bed. The open side should face up.

Construct the outer blankets of the bed. Use double-sided tape on the large tab to secure.

Slide the bed inside the blankets.

Construct the legs of the bed.

Glue the legs to the corners of the bottom side of the blankets. Stand the bed upright.

Use double-sided tape to attach the headboard to the end of the bed.

Use a small piece of double-sided tape on each side of the pillow. Remember to fluff it!

Attach the arms to the body of the sleepy sloth.

Aw, he's so tired. Sshh, let's let him sleep.

GOOD-BYE
BUT ONLY FOR A LITTLE WHILE

Awww! It is the end of our adventure! I will miss you, but don't be sad. We'll be together again before you know it! So long for now, friend!

DIRECTIONS:

1. Cut each of the letters on the solid yellow lines. If you have one, use a ⅛" hole punch to punch the holes.
2. Weave twine through the holes as shown.
3. Tie loops at the ends of the twine so you can hang your sign.
4. Hang and enjoy! So long!

WHAT YOU NEED:

- Scissors
- Twine

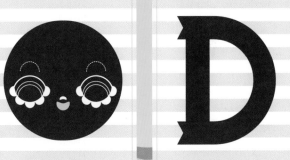

PAPER WONDERLAND BONUS WEBSITE!

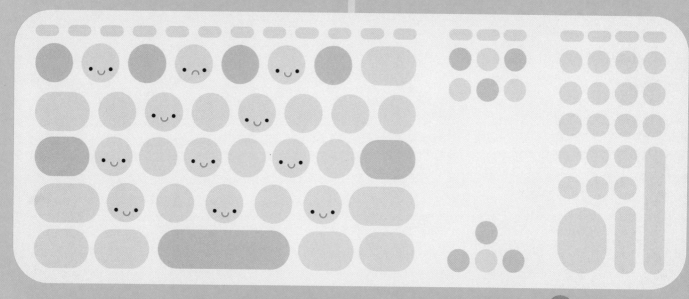

www.crowdedteeth.com/paperwonderland

Visit the Paper Wonderland website
for more free toy templates
and paper craft ideas!

Or visit www.crowdedteeth.com
for general info and updates!

MORE GREAT TITLES FROM HOW BOOKS!

KAWAII NOT

What exactly is kawaii? Well, *kawaii* is the Japanese term for "cute" (as in, "look at the fuzzy kitten, he's so kawaii") and *not* is an English term meaning "not." Explore the darker side of cute with this fun collection of quirky comic strips. Each strip is perforated, so you can rip it out and give it to a friend or stick it on your fridge. Also includes stickers! Nothing is more kawaii than stickers… except maybe kittens… or kittens on stickers!

#Z1845, 208 pages, paperback, ISBN: 978-1-60061-076-9

URBAN PAPER

This is a collection of 26 of the coolest designer paper toys, ready to be cut out and built. Each paper toy has step-by-step instructions (complete with easy-to-use diagrams) so even a novice will be able to make amazing paper toys with the help of an x-acto knife and a few dabs of glue. The DVD includes all 26 toy templates in PDF format, unabridged interviews with all the designers in the book and 33 bonus templates. So grab your scissors, your glue and your imagination, and get ready to enter an inspiring new world of paper toys!

#Z2231, 160 pages, paperback with DVD, ISBN: 978-1-60061-123-0

 These books and many others can be found at your local bookstore or at www.mydesignshop.com.